I0004605

MANAGING THIRD-PARTY SUPPLIER SOFTWARE QUALITY

TONY SIMMS CITP

Managing Third-Party Supplier Software Quality

COPYRIGHT

First published in Great Britain in 2012

Text and Images Copyright © Tony Simms (2012)

All rights reserved. No part of this publication may be reproduced, stored in a retrieval system or transmitted in any form or by any means without the prior permission in writing of the author nor be circulated in writing of any publisher, nor be otherwise circulated in any form of binding or cover other than that in which it is published without a similar condition including this condition, being imposed on the subsequent purchaser.

ABOUT THE AUTHOR

 I am the Principal Consultant at Roque Consulting and have provided project and software quality management services to companies and organisations such as BT, The BBC, The NHS, NSPCC and Siemens.

Since 1995 I has been involved in managing large software development programmes and projects, often requiring the management of third party software development. These projects have involved both green site systems development and the upgrade or migration of existing or commercial off the shelf systems.

This book is based on over fifteen years' worth of test management experience. In producing this book and in formulating this approach, many people have influenced my thinking, reviewed and improved my documents and contributed their own ideas. In large part this book builds on that work by others and I owe them a debt of gratitude.

My aim in producing this book is provide a guide to others in developing their own approach to managing third-parties. The book is not meant to be 'ready to wear' or 'one size fits all', rather by giving examples and setting out my approach, the reader will be able to pick and adapt the sections they require to meet their particular needs.

You can contact me via email at; Tony@roque.co.uk

Get a copy of the contract clauses

A number of people have commented on how helpful the contract clauses shown in this book have been. If after reading this book you also find them helpful and would like a 'MS Word' copy of them to use in your own organisation then please leave an honest review (good or bad) for the book on Amazon and then email me at

ContractClauses@roque.co.uk,

and I will send you a free copy of the clauses in word format.

INTRODUCTION

Software is big business, the right application, system or website can quite literally make a company, get it wrong and it can become the stuff of tabloid headlines Billions are spent every month by governments and companies on new software development projects, and many of these go to outside companies and contractors. Yet despite spending vast amounts on project management and development methodologies, many projects still over spend, deliver late and fail to include all expected functionality. More and more test managers are being forced out from the test department and in to the vendor's office to ensure that the supplier is delivering what is expected. By ensuring both the contractual terms and the relationship with the supplier are right, test and acceptance managers can make a significant contribution to ensuring the quality and suitability of the delivery from third-parties.

The relationship between the supplier's development team and the client's QA or test department can have a major impact on the success or failure of a project. In the best examples, the two teams work as one, co-operate well and respect each other's view, in the worse examples, the teams can be barely uttering a civil word to each other and every meeting becomes a battle with little ground lost or won. It is worth remembering that although each side has a different set of priorities, generally speaking, they all want the same outcome. Testers are familiar with the development/test 'V' model, and a similar model might illustrate where each party is coming from and what they are trying to achieve.

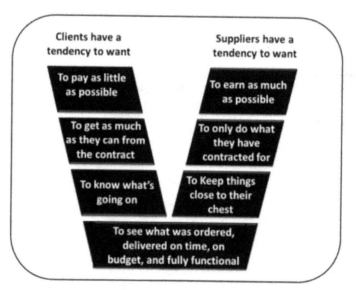

The Client / Third-party Supplier V Model

This book examines the principles and procedures applied to a number of large projects that required careful management of the third-party supplier. The testing contractual obligations and the management processes can be adapted and applied to managing third-party deliverables on projects of all sizes.

It covers:

- The need to manage third-parties
- What third parties can be expected to provide
- The importance of getting the contract right

THE NEED TO MANAGE THIRD-PARTIES

'Third-parties' can refer to;

- **Suppliers,** independent, external companies delivering software to you
- **Sub-Contractors,** companies or teams that are external to the main contractor, but are part of the 'internal' development team
- **Clients,** the end customer to whom the software is being delivered

The book concentrates on suppliers, though the principals and methods described can apply to across all third-parties.

Suppliers

Left to their own devices, many suppliers have the tendency to go into what I call *'Red October'* mode. In the movie *'The Hunt for Red October'*, the Soviet submarine commander, Ramius, (played by Sean Connery), is hunted by both the Soviet and US navy. Everyone knows the sub is out there, they know where it is heading, but until it surfaces no one knows where it is, how far it has travelled, which course it is following and quite what to expect when it surfaces. When something goes wrong with the engine there is a loud noise, plenty of shouting, a dramatic explosion and all the 'big wigs' get very excited.

Here's a secret: most supplier Project Managers secretly think they are Sean Connery! They don't want you to see what's going on. They hope that they can start the project, work away in isolation and deliver the solution at the end, with as little 'interference' as possible from the customer. The attitude appears to be: "Problems? Yes, of course there are problems, but as long as we sort them before the customer finds out, what's the issue?"

The issue, of course, is that if the problem is not sorted before the delivery date, then the solution is late, or defective, or over budget. Either way, the client has little time to take mitigating action and is often then held to ransom. I actually heard one project manager, faced with the fact that he could not deliver to my customer the promised solution on time, say:

"It's not good, and they won't like it, but what can they do, it's too late in the day for them to go elsewhere, they can shout and scream, but we have them over a barrel."

To avoid surprises and ensure we are not held to ransom we need to know the status of the project at each stage of its journey. We can't wait for the big disaster to hit and then look surprised and upset. We have to be able to measure progress at appropriate stages, report back to our managers and decide on appropriate action.

Subcontractors

Theoretically there should be a lower level of problems with subcontractors, as effectively they are 'part of the team'. In practice however, subcontractors can be the hardest group to manage. Subcontractors have a double reason to keep their processes hidden from the main contractor's Test Managers. Not only do they have the same pressure as a supplier, they have the added pressures that they have two clients breathing down their necks: the main contractor and the end customer). They may also be concerned that the contractor will try and steal their IP in order to provide the services themselves direct. Subcontractors also frequently feel, with some justification, that the main contractor blames them for all issues and delays that are really the fault of the main contractor.

Clients

Increasingly, contracts allow for the client to witness the testing undertaken by the supplier. It is therefore vital that expectations are set correctly and boundaries clearly understood. I was once in the position of having the client Assurance Manager refuse to sign off the Disaster Recovery test results, as we had not physically destroyed a server! The requirement was for a catastrophic failure of the server and the test involved pulling the cables on a running machine. Try as we might, we could not persuade the guy to accept the test, even though his own Test Manager agreed that the test was as valid as it could get.

As Test Managers we need to be in control of all test activities. If the client has the right to witness our testing, we need to be in control of that as well if we are to avoid deadlock, or worse still, complete mayhem, with the client imposing unscheduled, unscripted and unrealistic extra tests.

General Points

As test and QA professionals, we spend our time looking for faults, omissions, errors and non-compliance. We have a natural instinct to seek and expose. If your third-party counterpart is also a good Test Manager, they will welcome your input as long as it is tactful and well meaning.

Wherever possible your management should be 'invisible'. You should be working as a 'team member', providing extra input and guidance, offering fast turnaround of reviews and comments on documentation, plans and reports.

If things do go wrong and you are unable to influence the supplier to act in the way you require, you need to have a clear escalation route and process. You need to be able to push clear accurate and timely information up a level and know that it will be effectively and efficiently handled.

You need to establish your role in managing third-parties early on. If joining at the beginning of the project, ensure you have input into the contract and write your own Test Strategy to make your role clear and documented. If joining late, remember that the third-party has no idea who you are. You are free to present yourself as you wish so make sure that early on, in the first week or two you take time to set the ground rules with your third-party Test Manager. Make it clear that it does not matter what has gone before, you are here now, this is the way you do things, and this is the way you want him to do things.

WHAT YOU SHOULD EXPECT FROM SUPPLIERS

In order to understand and manage the supplier's deliverables, it is essential that there is an agreed and minimum level of information that the supplier is obliged to supply to the client's Test Manager. It is also essential that these are detailed in the contract and that it is subject to client approval.

Test Strategy

A Test Strategy is an absolute requirement. The Test Strategy is the first port of call for the 'what, where, when, how and by whom' information about testing, it is the point of reference by which all test activity is judged. You should ensure that nothing in the supplier's test strategy contradicts anything in your own strategy (if it exists)

The supplier's Test Strategy should cover the following components as a minimum:
- A description of the approach the supplier will be taking
- The requirements and objectives of the testing
- Which test phases are undertaken and by whom
- High level plan for the test activities
- Details of the test team organisation with key contact details
- What will be included in the test plans, specifications and scripts
- How requirements traceability will be managed
- How test results will be captured
- How test issues will be captured, reported and managed
- How progress will be managed and reported
- How tests will be executed
- What test metrics will be supplied
- What entry, suspension, resumption and exit criteria will be used
- Configuration management
- What test data will be used
- Which test environments will be used
- What testing tools will be used
- What test management tools will be used
- Approach to release management
- Any dependencies affecting the testing, including reliance on third-parties
- Test Plans, Specifications and Scripts

Depending on the size and complexity of the project there may be a separate Test Plan. Specification and Scripts for each phase of testing, or these may be combined in a single document. Their purpose is to take the Test Strategy and deconstruct it into detailed actions appropriate to each specific phase.

Regardless of the format (separate or combined) the following information needs to be provided.

Test Plans

Test plans should include;

- Any assumptions made that may impact upon testing
- An overview of the specific testing approach for the release and applicable test phase
- A detailed process for testing the applicable phase
- Details of the testing environment to be used
- The scope of the testing for the version or release, including a description of the sub-systems or functional areas under test
- List of requirements, change requests, or fixes to be tested
- Details of any deviations from the Test Strategy with a rationale for the differences
- Any specific dependencies, pre-requisites, assumptions and risks
- Details of the test scripts to be executed
- A description of the test data to be used for testing

Test specifications

Test specifications (if separate from the plans) should include;

- A detailed schedule for the testing
- The Test Criteria with a reference back to any requirements documentation or technical or design specifications
- A set of Test Scenarios designed to exercise all the Test Criteria identified within the Test Specification each with a reference to the Test Criteria covered by the Test Scenario
- A set of Test Scripts corresponding to the Test Scenarios describing the purpose of the test, the data requirements, any pre-requisites, the actions to be taken during the test, and the expected results for each step or action

Test Reports

Test reports are a critical piece of documentation, essential if you are to have a definitive reference point for approving the application or solution to proceed to the next step. Test reports should include at least the following information:

- Full details of the testing carried out
- Results of the testing
- Details of any deviation from the test strategy, plan and/or specification
- Details of if the testing failed in any way along with the extent and cause of the failure
- Summary metrics on issues and defects that have been raised
- Details of any outstanding errors, defects or issues, including a reference to the issue management log
- Details of any workarounds required as a result of any outstanding errors, defects or issues.

Work-Off Plans

If the Supplier fails to meet the acceptance criteria there may be good reason to allow them to move forward to the next stage. In such circumstances, the Supplier should provide a work-off plan detailing how the unresolved items will be addressed and risks mitigated. Work-off Plans should include:

- Details of all outstanding defects
- The severity and criticality of each defect, with any workarounds where appropriate
- Details of all mitigating actions
- The target dates for correction and testing of outstanding defects
- The target dates for release of software to correct the deficiency

THIRD PARTY MANAGEMENT TECHNIQUES

Reporting

Progress reporting is one of the most powerful tools in your armoury for managing suppliers; however it is also one of the hardest to get right. Every Test Manager has their own favourite set of reports and mechanism for reporting.

Test Reports

Test reports should give a detailed view of all testing carried out to date, including the number of scripts run, steps that have passed or failed, and where possible these should be linked to requirements to show coverage. Obviously if the Supplier is using a test management tool (Test Director, Silk Central, etc.) then this is a 'no brainer' and there should be no issue in requiring the weekly updates, or better still, obtaining your own login to run reports as and when you see fit. If not using a standard test management tool, then it is time to introduce the Supplier to Excel or one of the open source and cheap test management tools found on the internet.

There should be weekly and end of phase test reports. The time needed to produce the final end of phase test report can be substantially reduced by ensuring that the weekly test reports contain the information you will require in the final report.

The final test report should include the following sections;

- Executive Summary; This should provide a one page high level view of testing. The kinds of questions it should answer include:
- Was it completed?
- Did it finish on time?
- Were all test criteria met?
- How many severity 1 2 3 etc. issues raised?
- How many closed?

Test Scripts Results Summary

This should list all test scripts associated with the phase and detail how many steps were planned, how many run and how many passed or failed. Any explanation that will help the reader understand the results should also be given here

Test Issue Summary

This should list all test issues raised within this test phase against individual test scripts/specifications. It should also list the current status of issues raised. Any explanation that will help the reader understand the results should also be given here.

Detailed Testing Results

This section should give details of all testing carried out including: scripts run, steps passed failed, requirements satisfied. It should include:

- Details of all testing environments used
- Lists of the Tests run
- Impact assessments for of the outstanding Test Issues
- Lists of requirements impacted by failed Test cases
- Lists of requirements impacted by 'Not Run' Test Cases
- All Test Issues and observations raised during Testing
- Overall Impact Assessment

This section should give a detailed assessment of the overall impact on the system of the issues detailed above and answer such questions as: Is the system fit to go live with work rounds? Are there critical issues that need to be addressed?

Test Issue Resolution Plan

This section should detail how the issues raised will be addressed and managed to a conclusion.

Progress Reports

Progress reports (as opposed to test reports) should give you not only an idea of progress against milestone, but also details of any risk and issues as well as actions to mitigate those risks. The purpose is to ensure that you have a clear understanding of the true state of the project. If you understand the project progress, slippage and issues you can intervene to help or make suggestions before it's too late. Bear in mind that your job is not to catch the supplier out, but to ensure they deliver. If necessary, issues can be escalated to the next level.

Progress reports should always be challenged and not taken on face value. It is not acceptable to be told five weeks on the trot all is going to plan and then to be suddenly told the week before the deadline that the project has slipped two weeks. I use a simple technique of mapping a limited number of milestones, (e.g. requirements documented and signed off, test criteria mapped to requirements, test script X written, etc.) for each requested milestone target date, each week I ask if the target date has changed. If the date has slipped, I ask for the issue that has caused the slippage to be detailed. For each Issue I as for the actions that will be performed to mitigate the slippage. I also ask each week, what was achieved this week against what was planned for the week, and what is planned for next week.

Reviewing

In the UK we have a tradition of 'fair play' and sportsmanship for example you can't shoot a pheasant on the ground, it has to be in flight, police are not allowed by law to hide speed cameras, they have to be in plain sight and proceeded by a large warning sign. Unfair conduct is simply 'not cricket' in the UK. Reviewing is the Test Manager's version of fair play.

The purpose of reviewing supplier documentation, processes and procedures is to give due and fair notice of errors, omissions and failings in advance of when it really matters. That way when the final document is presented and it has not addressed your comments, it is 'fair game' and 'open season' to go hunting. Then, quite rightly, you can get on your moral high horse and explain in exasperated tones why, exactly, they need to redo this piece of work and why they will not be issued an authority to proceed until it's done.

In order to make this process as fair as possible I do three things:

I go through the contractual requirements for each document and produce a check list which I provide to the supplier. (We have to play fair, remember.)

I offer to hold an informal undocumented page turn with the author prior to first submission. (I usually get a draft before the page turn, but it is not recorded as a delivery). I detail all the things I would have commented on if this was a formal review. This gives the author the opportunity to ask questions and to fully understand what is required. At this stage it is also possible that there is an area with which the supplier will be unable to comply. I will usually discuss mitigating actions with the author and suggest that these are included under the relevant section of the document

For all formal deliveries I always provide formal written comments, which are stored in the project office repository and tracked. It is not unheard of for some of these comments eventually finding themselves on the general project Risks & Issues list.

Witnessing

There can be no substitute for actually sitting alongside the testers and witnessing what is going on. Is the environment set up correctly? Are scripts being followed or are tests being ticked off without thought? Are issues being found but not reported, or worse still, fixed on the fly? These are all questions it is very difficult to answer by reading reports. Witnessing allows you not only to ask the question, but see, real time, the answer.

The amount of involvement a witness will have in the process will vary from contract to contract, however the following provides a good basis for agreeing the scope of the witness responsibilities and authority:

The test witness will be suitably qualified for the aspect of the testing they are witnessing;

The supplier will allow preparatory discussions and review with the test witness to be incorporated into the review of the Test Specification or Scripts before the start of testing;

The witness will not be involved in the execution of any test, however they may request an explanation of particular activity, ask for evidence relating to a particular element, comment upon the execution of a test or ask for a test to be repeated if not satisfied that it has been correctly undertaken;

The witness may elect at any time to witness all or only some elements of any Test being undertaken and the supplier will provide reasonable assistance and access to enable them to do so;

The witness will verify that the Supplier has conducted the Tests in accordance the Test Criteria and the relevant Test Plan and Test Specification;

The witness may produce and deliver ad hoc reports on those elements they have witnessed.

The witness may raise Test Issues on the Test Issues Management Log in respect of any Testing witnessed;

Milestone Check Points

As detailed above the milestone check points are contractual 'stop and think' opportunities. Without the check points it is easy to recognise that an element of the project is unacceptable, for example, lacking server build documentation, but then simply plough on with every good intention of doing it later. The issue is that as more and more items get added to the snag list, there is never time (or incentive) to address them, there is always a more pressing priority. This simply stores all the issues for a final showdown at a very late stage.

In terms of managing the supplier, the key to milestone checkpoints is making it clear that any progress beyond this point, without the Authority to Proceed certificate is not recognised by the client, and will not attract payment. That is not to say that if the failed elements of the last milestone are adequately addressed in a timely fashion, the later progress will not be accepted, it simply means that until the last milestone has been met, all this subsequent work is at risk. For example, in one of my projects, we had witnessed the successful completion of testing and were happy to sign off the end of phase test report. The report was required before the next stage of testing could officially start, and the start of the next stage (OAT) attracted a stage payment. However the same resource from the Supplier was required to lead OAT as well as produce the report. The timetable was such that the OAT took priority and the stage report was six weeks late, as was the payment, but the OAT completed on time and was granted a retrospective ATP.

Staged Payments

It's essential that stage payments are both enforced and flexible. Requiring completion of a stage before payment certainly concentrates the supplier's mind and gives you a very big carrot to dangle just out of reach until all requirements have been met. On the other hand, it is no good withholding payment if that will jeopardise the financial viability of the supplier (particularly true of smaller suppliers, but also true when the stage payments are late in the project and represent some hundreds of millions as in the case of some of the larger government projects I have been on).

In addition to specifying the acceptance criteria that trigger the payment, it may also be useful to specify 'claw back' criteria in the result of a failure to deliver. For example, if the delivery of an automated process on time requires the client to continue to employ extra staff to undertake a manual process, that may justify a repayment of a certain amount from an earlier payment to offset the clients additional costs.

THE CONTRACT

Suppliers are only obliged to do what they are contracted to do and often they want to do as little as possible, for as much as possible and want to get paid, as quickly as possible. This is what drives their activity. If the test report is a contractual delivery and payment depends on it being signed off then by and large, you can expect to get a test report. If the test report is not a contractual delivery, then you will be hard pressed to insist on it if the supplier has have no incentive or capacity to provide it; to them it is simply extra 'nice to have' documentation. This is true of every stage of testing. There is no end to the reasons given by suppliers who may not be motivated to undertake full and vigorous QA and testing.

There is sometimes a contention between different departments within the supplier's organisation. There may be internal cost centre battles with one budget 'pot' allocated from the contract to development and another to support. If the development department can obtain sign off of the delivery at an earlier stage, they may well choose to do so. The logic is: *'I've done my bit on time and within budget, if there is more to put right, that's now a support issue - let them pay for it'.* This may be a little crudely worded, but it is not an uncommon situation. There may also be an added bonus to the supplier if that delivery triggers a stage payment and subsequent support work carries opportunities to charge.

The supplier may have an adequate development team, but no resource for testing or documentation. I have actually been told by one failing supplier's head of QA that I needed

".....to understand that our developers are not like other suppliers, they are world class and therefore there is not a need for a full test regime."

In fact they were already late, unable to deliver full functionality and were severely over budget. As their development went into overspend cutting the testing regime was seen as a way to limit costs.

If test procedures, reports, acceptance criteria and anything else you require are not agreed in the contract, it may be difficult to argue later that a release should be rejected because it is not fit for purpose or lacking documentation. This is particularly true when, although the system appears to be working, there is little or no support or operational documentation and no reports or metrics to give you confidence that it has been adequately tested.

The key benefits of getting the contract right are:

- The ability to detail exactly what testing should be undertaken
- The ability to dictate the makeup of each document

- The ability to state what review and influence of their testing you will be entitled to
- The ability to fix checkpoints linked to 'Authority To Proceed' certificates and staged payments
- The ability to state penalties and consequences of failure to deliver any obligation

Main Test Related Clauses to Consider:

Definitions

It is important that right from the outset that the client and the supplier are using the same language. It may seem a little over the top to define 'Regression Testing', but when dealing with contractual terms such definitions are essential and will only reveal their worth when things go wrong. At that point there needs to be no room for doubt or manoeuvre. You may be clear what everyone should understand by "System Integration Testing", but don't assume that the supplier shares the same view. An added bonus of making sure that you have all your key terms in the definition is that you then have a checklist for the test element of the contract.

Processes and Procedures

It is amazing how quickly all the sales talk about the supplier following this or that methodology or QA process evaporates in the heat generated by an over worked development team, tied into unrealistic targets and a finite budget. In fact I am constantly surprised by how upfront and open suppliers are about the worth of a presales promise, with supplier contracts often stating that the contract is the whole sum of the agreement and nothing previously communicated, verbally or in writing, form any part of the agreement. The time to insist on good test and QA process is before the contract is signed and only if it is incorporated in the contract can you then moan if things do not go the way you want them.

Documentation

Full, clear and accurate documentation is the most powerful tool in your management armoury. It allows you to understand and comment on testing long before the first test step is run. It allows you to track progress, validate milestones and justify promoting test deliverables to the next stage. Finally, if the documentation is well done and everything else fails, it is the unemotional, empirical, quantifiable and traceable argument for placing responsibility where it belongs: client or supplier, or a mix of both. On a number of occasions I have had the gratifying satisfaction of seeing the opposition's legal team get more and more uncomfortable as they are faced with page after page of evidence which demonstrates that their client may not have given them quite the right picture and all their carefully rehearsed arguments are not going to hold water.

Witnessing

The ability to get in amongst the suppliers' troops and watch what is going on, offering guidance where necessary and gaining a real feel for the quality of the application and the process is invaluable to you as a Test Managers. If played correctly, witnessing will also be seen as being a great benefit by the supplier. However, gaining entry in is the challenge. Most suppliers' reaction if you ask to come in and witness what's going on will either be suspicion or rejection. They are worried that you will:

take up too much time, asking stupid questions and stopping people getting on with their work

- write a critical report and cause trouble
- ask them to do more than they are prepared to do and
- talk to developers. (I am never sure why this one comes up, but it always does!)

In reality, the motivation for witnessing is simply to make sure they are doing what they have agreed to do, help them to get what they are doing right and to gain a level of confidence about the application long before it hits the release note stage. Getting the right to witness in to the contract can reduce the need for a lot of painful meetings, 'tiptoeing around' and cajoling.

Milestones and Staged Payments

By agreeing milestones, with clear acceptance criteria, certification and stage payments you maintain control of the project. Obviously how many of the milestones are linked to payments and how much each payment is worth will vary according to the circumstance of each client and supplier. However I would suggest that as a minimum, no more than a third of the contract value should be payable in advance, a third at a later stage (M5?) and the final payment only after an initial operations review or a bedding-in period.

Each milestone should have clear acceptance criteria associated with it. To move from one milestone on to the next stage, the milestone acceptance criteria needs to be shown to have been met and an Authority To Proceed (ATP) or Acceptance Certificate issued to confirm that the supplier is now able to move to the next stage. Suppliers may wish to move on to the next stage before receiving an ATP but do so at their own risk.

Example Milestones

M1. Implementation Planning

This milestone allows you to review the enabling documentation for the project, the Quality Plan and Implementation Plan. It allows you to make sure that at least the intentions are right before too much work is undertaken.

M2. Design Complete

This milestone allows functional and technical specifications; test documentation, elements required for Escrow and all documentation deliverables to be reviewed and agreed. It also gives a chance to validate the solution proposed by the supplier.

M3. Start of Systems Integration Testing

This milestone allows you the opportunity to ensure that earlier stages of testing have been completed successfully, and that all severity 1 or 2 issues have been addressed, and remaining issues are within the entry criteria. In addition it enables you to ensure that the correct test environments are available and that before testing starts, the Test Plans and Specifications are acceptable and signed off.

M4. Start of System Testing

Again, this milestone allows you to ensure all that has gone before has been completed successfully and all is in place before the next stage starts.

M5. Start of Ready for Service Testing

This milestone allows you to ensure all that has gone before has been completed successfully and all is in place before the next stage starts. It should include checks that all Operational Processes and Procedures are complete, documented and acceptable and that build, install and configuration documentation provides all necessary information for these activities.

M6. Ready for Service

This milestone allows you to determine that all the elements required to run a successful system are in place before the system goes live:

M7. Initial Operations Review

Final payment should ideally follow a 'running in period' this allows post go live activity to be monitored and Management Information and Service Level reports to be analysed. Holding back the final payment also adds incentive to the supplier to fix any real life issues as soon as possible.

EXAMPLE CONTRACT CLAUSES

Contracts may be single documents, or consist of multiple parts, (for example a specific test Schedule a single document or not, the main test related elements detailed below should be covered somewhere.

Definitions Clause

In this contract, unless the context otherwise requires, the following words shall have the following meanings:

"Authority to Proceed Certificate" means the notification granted by the CLIENT pursuant to this Contract materially in the form set out at Appendix XXX;

"Certificate" means an Authority to Proceed Certificate or a Milestone Achievement Certificate as applicable;

"Deployment Testing" means the Testing of the design, installation and configuration of the SOLUTION and Testing of any data migrated to the SOLUTION

"Deployment Verification" means the verification that the operation and performance of the SOLUTION conforms to the CLIENT's Requirements and the Contractor's Technical Solution;

"Deployment Verification Criteria" means the criteria necessary to establish Deployment Verification;

"Integration Testing" means the end-to-end integration Testing, including Testing of interfaces between the SOLUTION and any relevant CLIENT applications as further described in XXX;

"Module Testing" (Unit Testing) means the Testing of functionality for each unit/module within SOLUTION,

"Milestone Achievement Certificate" means a certificate issued by the CLIENT substantially in the form of a document set out in Appendix XXX;

"Ready for Operations Testing" (Ready for Service Testing) means the Testing of operational support processes as further described in XXX;

"Regression Testing" means the testing to ensure that existing functionality is not affected by the addition of new and modified functionality;

"System Testing" means the Testing of the SOLUTION as a whole, or in part,

"Test Criteria" means the criteria necessary to demonstrate compliance of the SOLUTION Services (or an element thereof) with the CLIENT's Requirements, including in respect of the CLIENT's Requirements, the Service Level Specifications and Performance Monitoring, Security Requirements, the SUPPLIERS's Technical Solution, together with any amendments to the SUPPLIERS's Technical Solution agreed subsequently with the CLIENT (such agreement not to be unreasonably withheld or delayed) pursuant to the Change Control Procedure, and any requirements of an agreed Change;

"Tests" means the tests performed to ensure that the SOLUTION complies with the Test Criteria, including Integration Testing, Regression Testing, Deployment Testing, Deployment Verification and System Testing;

"Test Issue" means an issue identified during Testing, including whereby any relevant Test Criteria is or are not met;

"Test Issue Level" means the level of severity allotted to a Test Issue in accordance with the levels set out in XXX;

"Test Issue Management Log" means the single centralised tool with multiple user access where the SUPPLIER records and tracks all Test Issues relating to the delivery of the SOLUTION;

"Test Plan" means the plan for the conduct of Tests in respect of each Milestone;

"Test Specification" means the specification setting out how the Tests will demonstrate that the Test Criteria have been met

"Test Strategy" means the Test Strategy in existence pursuant to this Agreement;

"Test Witnesses" means those persons appointed as such in accordance with paragraph XXX of the contract;

"Test Witnessing" means those activities undertaken by the Test Witness, including observing, verifying, reviewing and reporting on Tests;

"Usability Testing" means Testing of the day-to-day use of the SOLUTION

"Work-off Plan" means the plan developed to resolve any Test Issues arising during Testing.

Testing Procedure And Process Clause

Milestones are detailed in Annex XXX. The SUPPLIER shall ensure that it provides such reasonable assistance and support as is required by the CLIENT, to enable the SOLUTION to undergo and complete successful Testing detailed for each Milestone, before the Milestone Dates agreed between the parties and set out in the relevant Detailed SOLUTION Implementation Plan.

The CLIENT will determine the precise timing of the Testing in discussion with the SUPPLIER as part of the agreement process for the relevant Detailed SOLUTION Implementation Plan.

Except for Usability Testing (for which the SUPPLIER will be required to provide reasonable support to the CLIENT), the SUPPLIER will be responsible for the conduct of all Testing.

All Tests will be conducted in accordance with;

the Test Strategy
the Test Plans and the Test Specifications relevant to each Milestone and
in respect of the SOLUTION Deployment, the Deployment Verification Criteria

The Testing to be carried out in respect of each Milestone such Testing as is reasonably necessary to determine whether the SOLUTION satisfies the CLIENT's Requirements and is otherwise in accordance with this Agreement.

The SUPPLIER shall not submit any part of the SOLUTION for Testing:

until the parties have agreed the Test Plan, and the Test Specification or the Deployment Verification Criteria (as applicable) and
unless it has provided the CLIENT with a written notice certifying that the SOLUTION is ready for Testing.

At the end of each day of Testing, the SUPPLIER shall record the summary outcome of the Tests conducted during that day and shall notify the CLIENT's Project Manager in writing of the success or failure of each Test.

The SUPPLIER shall also notify the CLIENT as soon as reasonably practicable and in any event no later than five (5) days after the occurrence of any such failures or errors, of any failures or errors of which the SUPPLIER becomes aware during the course of any Test.

Upon receipt of any such notice of a failure or error, the CLIENT may inspect the element of the SOLUTION Service to which the failure or error relates (including any associated Software and/or underlying materials) at such time as it shall require, but in any event within fourteen (14) days of the receipt of such notice of a failure or error.

The SUPPLIER shall carry out Regression Testing for all appropriate components of the SOLUTION where functionality is delivered in phases and also by agreement of the parties as and when required pursuant to the Change Control Procedure.

In respect of any Milestone, the CLIENT shall review:

the interim versions (showing progress to date) of the Test Reports and the Test Issue Management Log at an agreed time prior to the completion of all relevant Testing and

the final versions of the Test Reports and the Test Issue Management Log at completion of the relevant Testing

Where any component of the SOLUTION has successfully completed the Tests by meeting the Test Criteria by the applicable Milestone (or revised Milestone, where applicable), the CLIENT will issue the relevant Certificate. The issue of a Certificate shall:

mean that the relevant Milestone has been successfully achieved and

shall act as a trigger for payment of any applicable Charges but

shall not act as confirmation that the SOLUTION meets the CLIENT's Requirements

Test Documentation Clause

Test Strategy

The SUPPLIER shall develop a SOLUTION specific Test Strategy for approval by the CLIENT as soon as practicable but in any case no later than sixty (60) days prior to the start date of the first scheduled Test. The Test Strategy shall include:

names and contact details of the SUPPLIER's relevant representatives

an overview of the Testing to be conducted in relation to the systems and solutions

an overview of how Testing will be conducted in relation to the types of Testing set out in Appendix XX Testing Regime

a plan for the Testing to be conducted in relation to each Milestone, including as a minimum where applicable

an overview of the Testing for that Milestone

the start date for the Testing

the Testing procedure, including the type of Test and the scope of the Testing

the Test objectives

the Test pre-requisites and the mechanism for measuring the pre-requisites

the Test completion criteria

the Testing mechanism

the intended volume and management of Test data

the timetable for each Test or group of Tests

a high level identification of the resources required for Testing, including
 - facilities,
 - infrastructure,
 - test Harness,
 - test Personnel,

- third-party involvement,
- other Integrated Service Provider's involvement,
- CLIENT involvement (to the extent such involvement may be required by the SUPPLIER),
- external systems,
- any business process to be simulated,
- plus the plan to make the resources available for Testing with lead times

the provision for ensuring consistency with the Integration Testing of any other relevant Integrated Service Provider

the process to be used to capture and record Test results and the method to process the Test results in order to establish their content

the method for mapping the expected Test results to the Test Criteria

the procedure to be followed should Test Criteria not be met or Test results fail to be as expected, including a rectification procedure

the procedure to be followed by the SUPPLIER (and the CLIENT and/or Test Witnesses as applicable) to sign off the Testing for each Milestone

the process for ensuring the quality of the Testing (e.g. review of Test results)

a procedure for logging Test results, Test Issues and categorisation of Test Issues and recording of the same in the Test Issue Management Log

the process for the production and maintenance of Test Reports and reporting templates for the Test Reports, the Test Issue Management Log, and Work-Off Plan and

the technical environments required to support the Test Strategy; and the procedure for managing the configuration of the Test environments

The CLIENT will approve or reject the Test Strategy within fourteen (14) days of its receipt. If the CLIENT rejects the Test Strategy it will provide within the same fourteen (14) day period written details of its reasons and require re-submission of the Test Strategy amended accordingly.

In the event that the CLIENT rejects the Test Strategy, the SUPPLIER shall re-submit the Test Strategy to the CLIENT within fourteen (14) days of receipt of the CLIENT's written rejection

In the event that the re-submitted Test Strategy Annex is not acceptable to the CLIENT (acting reasonably) then the matter shall be determined by the parties' respective Project Managers

Test Plan

The SUPPLIER shall provide a Test Plan for each Milestone for the approval of the CLIENT not less than thirty five (35) days prior to the start date for the Testing of the relevant Milestone.

The CLIENT will approve or reject each Test Plan within fourteen (14) days of its receipt from the SUPPLIER. If the CLIENT acting reasonably rejects the Test Plan it will provide details of its reasons for such rejection. The parties will use all reasonable endeavours to agree the Test Plan not less than twenty one (21) days prior to the start date for the Testing of the relevant Milestone and if not agreed within such time period the matter shall be determined by the parties' respective Project Managers.

Each Test Plan shall include as a minimum:

an overview of the purpose of the Test, the Milestone to which it relates, and the specific Test Criteria to be met

a detailed procedure for the Test and the type of Testing to be carried out

a detailed specification and scope for each Test or group of Tests

the timetable for each Test or group of Tests including start and end dates

the Testing mechanism and the extent to which it is equivalent to live operations

dates and methods by which the CLIENT can inspect Test results or witness the Tests in order to establish that the Test Criteria have been met

the specific mechanism to be used to capture and record Test results and the method to be used to process the results of the Tests to establish their content

the mechanism for ensuring the quality, completeness and relevance of the Tests

the format and an example of weekly Test progress reports and the process with which the CLIENT may access the daily Test schedules

the process within which the CLIENT will review process, incidents and progress and how the CLIENT will contribute to the classification of Test Issues

the Test program for each week of Testing;

the procedure to be followed by the SUPPLIER and by the CLIENT (to the extent the SUPPLIER may require the CLIENT's co-operation) prior to provision by the CLIENT of a Certificate

the process for maintenance of Test Reports and templates of the Test Reports to be provided at the end of the Testing of the Key Milestone

the anticipated procedure, including the timetable and the resources which would be required, for re-Testing and

the SUPPLIER's requirements of the CLIENT for access to data and Test messages

Test Specification

Following submission of a Test Plan, the SUPPLIER shall provide a Test Specification for the relevant stage of Testing for the approval of the CLIENT not less than twenty one (21) days prior to the start date for the Testing of the relevant

The CLIENT will approve or reject the Test Specification within fourteen (14) days of its receipt from the SUPPLIER. If the CLIENT rejects the Test Specification it will provide details of its reasons for such rejection. The parties will use all reasonable endeavours to agree the Test Specification not less than fourteen (14) days prior to the start date of the relevant Tests and if not agreed within such time period the matter shall be determined by the parties' respective Project Managers.

Each Test Specification shall include as a minimum:

the specification of the Test data, including its
- source,
- scope,
- volume and management,
- a request (if applicable) for relevant Test data to be provided by the CLIENT and
- the extent to which it is equivalent to live operational data

identification of the resources (in respect of both the CLIENT and the SUPPLIER) required for the Test, such as:
- premises,
- equipment and
- facilities
- infrastructure
- test harness
- CLIENT or CLIENT Service Recipient involvement
- test personnel
- third-parties
- external systems; and
- any business process to be simulated (if applicable),that may be required for the Testing (including any third-parties, resources, systems and equipment), which must have been confirmed prior to the submission of the Test Specification to the CLIENT;

a plan to make the resources available for Testing and, unless otherwise reasonably requested, a summary of the agreements made with SUPPLIER Parties, third-parties or external system providers to provide resources for the Test;

test objectives and expected Test results, including
- a mechanism to be used to capture and record Test results
- a method to process the Test results to establish their content
- test pre-requisites and the mechanism for measuring them
- mapping of the expected Test results to the Test Criteria and
- test scripts

Test Witnessing Clause

Test Witnessing includes the following elements:

the Contractor will allow preparatory discussions and review with the Test Witnesses to be incorporated into the review of the Test Specification or Testing Quality Audit process where appropriate

the CLIENT will, in accordance with the Expected Standard, provide appropriately skilled personnel for Test Witnessing

the CLIENT Representatives will review Test documentation and will attend and engage in the performance of SOLUTION demonstrations to enable the CLIENT to gain an informed view of whether an outstanding Test Issue may be closed or should be re-Tested. The CLIENT Representatives may elect at any time to witness elements of any Test being undertaken and the SUPPLIER shall provide all reasonable assistance and access to the CLIENT Representative to enable them to do so

the Test Witness(es) will be given reasonable access to all relevant documentation and Testing environments by the SUPPLIER

the Test Witness(es) will verify that the SUPPLIER has conducted the Tests in accordance with the Test Criteria and the relevant Test Plan and Test Specification

the Test Witness(es) will not be involved in the execution of any Test but may request evidence relating to it or to comment upon its execution

the Test Witness(es) may produce and deliver ad hoc reports on those elements of Testing which the relevant Test Witness has witnessed to the SUPPLIER and the CLIENT for information purposes only, and these may be used by the CLIENT to assess whether the Tests have been achieved

the Test Witness(es) may raise Test Issues on the Test Issues Management Log in respect of any Testing

the SUPPLIER must demonstrate to the relevant Test Witness, who attend the Testing, that adequate modifications and Testing as reasonably determined by the SUPPLIER, have been performed leading to closure of the Test Issue by the Test Witnes; and

the Test Witness (es) may influence significantly the assessment and approval (or otherwise) by the CLIENT of the Test Issue Level and whether the CLIENT grants or refuses to grant a Certificate

Milestones Clause

Development and Implementation Phase Milestones

The SUPPLIER shall achieve the following Milestones during the Development and Implementation Phase by the corresponding Milestone Dates set out in Appendix XXX:

M1. Implementation Planning

SUPPLIER to have achieved Notice of Approval from the CLIENT in relation to the following Documentation:

(A) Quality Plan

(B) Implementation Plan

M2. Design Complete

SUPPLIER to have achieved Notice of Approval from the CLIENT in relation to the following Documentation:

(A) Functional Specifications;

(B) Technical Specifications;

(C) Process Definition Deliverable;

(D) Test Strategy;

(E) Testing Requirements;

(F) Capacity Plan;

(G) Escrow Software List and;

(H) Documentation Deliverables List.

M3. Start of Systems Integration Testing

SUPPLIER to have achieved Notice of Approval from the CLIENT in relation to:

(A) Successful completion of all Tests referred to in paragraphs XXX to XXX of schedule X (Testing Regime) without any Severity 1 Issues or any Severity 2 Issues;

(B) Provision of Test Environments in accordance with the Test Strategy and relevant Test Plan; and

(C) The following Documentation:

(1) xxx Test Plans;

(2) xxx Test Specifications.

M4. Start of System Testing

SUPPLIER to have achieved Notice of Approval from the CLIENT in relation to:

(A) Systems Integration Testing, including but not limited to successful completion of all Tests referred to in paragraph xxx of schedule X (Testing Regime) regarding Systems Integration Testing;

(B) Infrastructure Testing of the SOLUTION including but not limited to successful completion of all Tests referred to in paragraph xxx of schedule X (Testing Regime) regarding Infrastructure Testing, and

(C) All documents referred to in paragraph xxx of schedule X (Testing Regime), approved by the CLIENT.

M 5. Start of Ready for Service Testing

SUPPLIER to have achieved Notice of Approval from The CLIENT in relation to:

(A) Infrastructure Proving, including but not limited to successful completion of all Tests referred to in paragraph xxx of schedule X (Testing Regime) regarding Infrastructure.

(B) Operational Processes and Procedures provided by the SUPPLIER comply with paragraph xxx of schedule X, are complete and acceptable to the CLIENT acting reasonably;

(C) Suitable Test environments provided for Testing of software releases prior to promotion to the operational environment, and

(D) All Documentation relevant to the Solution Infrastructure, including but not limited to: instructions and procedures for the build, installation, configuration and commissioning of the Infrastructure, including final 'as built' drawings, and

(E) Demonstration through Test Witnessing that the Documentation related to build, configuration and installation of Systems provides all necessary information for these activities to be carried out by a suitably skilled engineer without background knowledge of the Systems.

M6. Ready for Service

SUPPLIER to have achieved Notice of Agreement to Deploy from the CLIENT in relation to the following:

(A) Successful completion of all Tests referred to in paragraphs xxx of schedule X (Testing Regime) regarding Ready for Service Testing;

(B) Any Work-off Plan agreed with the CLIENT ;

(D) Full compliance with clause XXX in relation to Escrow Software; and

(D) The following Documentation:

- (1)   Asset Register;
- (2)   Exit Plan;
- (3)   Security Policy together with all associated Security procedures; and
- (4)   Disaster Recovery Plan, in accordance with the other provisions of the Agreement

M7. Initial Operations Review

Post Go Live date activity process checking, monitoring and MIS reporting shows that the PIs in schedule X are being met with Service Credit deductions for the Month following the Go Live date being no more than ten percent (10%) of the Charges for the Month.

General Milestone Terms

The parties acknowledge that for all Milestones after Milestone 1 the achievement criteria specified in the table above are high level and may, on a case-by-case basis require supplemental additional, low-level criteria ("Detailed Milestone Achievement Criteria").

Upon achievement of a Milestone (the "Achieved Milestone"), the parties shall use best efforts, in good faith, to promptly agree such Detailed Milestone Achievement Criteria as are appropriate to be applied in relation to the next Milestone to be achieved.

If no agreement on the Detailed Milestone Achievement Criteria is reached within twenty (20) Working Days of the date of achievement of the Achieved Milestone, unless the CLIENT agrees otherwise, the CLIENT shall, acting reasonably and in good faith, be entitled to determine what Detailed Milestone Achievement Criteria (if any) are required for the next Milestone.

CONCLUSION

A 2011 report from Geneca, entitled 'Doomed From The Start' states

75% of respondents admit that their projects are either always or usually "doomed right from the start," including 27% who always feel this way.

Simply appointing a supplier and hoping that they will turn up on time with an acceptable solution is a risky act of faith that has seen an ever increasing number of projects fail. Suppliers have a tendency to over promise and keep bad news away from the client for as long as possible. It is incumbent on the client to understand what the true state of affairs is, if they are to properly serve the interests of their stakeholders.

By understanding what you should be able to expect from a third party supplier, you are in a better place to agree up front what each parties role and responsibilities are.

Getting the contract right, so that you have an agreed level of access, deliverables, milestones and payments, allows both sides to understand, cost and manage the project in a way that maximises the chance of success.

Getting the management actions right so that you maintain the balance between being informed but not getting in the way is an essential part of the whole quality deliverable lifecycle.

If after reading this book you feel you might want to beef up your own organisations contract clauses around testing, then I am happy to send you a MSWord copy of the clauses used in this book. To get a copy please leave an honest review (good or bad) for the book on Amazon (It would help if you would give your role and organisation, e.g. Test Manager, Bugfinder Corp) and then email me at

ContractClauses@roque.co.uk,

to let me know and I will send you a copy.

###

www.ingramcontent.com/pod-product-compliance
Lightning Source LLC
Chambersburg PA
CBHW060936050326
40689CB00013B/3114